THE GOD WHO LOVES AND HATES

THE BOOK OF OBADIAH—WHY GOD LOVED JACOB AND HATED ESAU

Kevin Madison

Copyright ©2021 Kevin Madison

All rights reserved. This book or any portion thereof may not be reproduced or used in any manner whatsoever without the express written permission of the publisher except for the use of brief quotations in a book review.

ISBN: 978-1-7377003-6-4 paperback
ISBN: 978-1-7377003-7-1 ebook

Cover design and publishing assistance by The Happy Self-Publisher

Published by Madison Christian Books, LLC
Kevin J. Madison
Founder: Treasure in Every Verse Ministry
Owner: Madison Christian Books, LLC
925 S. Lewis St. #255
New Iberia, LA 70560
Website: kevinjmadison.com
Email: tevm9328@gmail.com

Table of Contents

Dedication v

Introduction vii

Chapter 1: Origin of Election 1

Chapter 2: The Son of Promise 7

Chapter 3: Historical View—Descendants of Esau.
 Who was Herod? 15

Chapter 4: Esau's Little Secret. 25

Chapter 5: A Rebel at Heart 35

Chapter 6: The Marriage From Hell 39

Chapter 7: Sleeping with the Enemy. 47

Chapter 8: The Purge and Promised Restoration. 51

Bibliography 61

About the Author. 63

Dedication

To all the pastors who have helped me grow in my walk with the Lord, whether in church attendance, on radio, or on television. I give thanks to the Lord God for you all.

To Pastors Carl Brown, Dr. John Barnett, John MacArthur, Robert Jeffers, my dad, the late Pastor Leroy Phillips, the late Pastors Dr. J. Vernon McGee and Adrian Rogers.

Introduction

Our journey commences in the beginning, no, not their beginning, in the beginning with the eternal God seeking the origin of His election. We find that a promise was given. What was this promise? Why was the promise decreed? To whom was it issued?

Along the route we visit an historical site and discovered that several descendants were kings. Who were they and over what nation? Later we discovered that the family patriarch had a secret. I wonder which type of secret. Could it be a mistress, an illegitimate child? Oh, maybe it's a murder mystery, do tell.

While visiting the historical site it was also learned that our patriarch had a mean streak, he was a rebel at heart. What did he do to earn such reputation? Could it be a result from a marriage because there were whispers concerning a marriage from hell?

As we were concluding our journey it was revealed that our patriarch and other members of the family were sleeping with the enemies. How can that be? Whom can you trust? It's lonesome being the king.

We finally arrive at our destination just in time to witness the purge. The purge!? What in the world is that and why is it necessary? Oh, now I see, it's the promised restoration. Whew, I love happy endings?

CHAPTER 1

ORIGIN OF ELECTION

Many people are shocked when they hear that the Bible states God hates certain people. They always question how a God of love can hate anyone. The Bible provides the answer to this question in several of its sixty-six books; however, there is an Old Testament book dedicated to this topic, the little book of Obadiah. The Lord provides great details concerning the election of Jacob and the rejection of Esau. Although Obadiah is not quoted much by other biblical authors, the judgment against Edom, in retrospect, is mentioned within several Old Testament books.

"[5] "For My sword shall be bathed in heaven; Indeed, it shall come down on Edom, And on the people of My curse, for judgment. [6] The sword of the LORD is filled with blood, It is made overflowing with fatness, With the blood of lambs and goats, With the fat of the kidneys of rams. For the LORD has a sacrifice in Bozrah, And a great slaughter in the land of Edom. [7] The wild oxen shall come down with them, And the young bulls with the mighty bulls; Their land shall be soaked with blood, and their dust saturated with fatness." [8] For it is the day of the LORD's vengeance, The year of recompense for the cause of Zion. [9] Its streams shall be turned into pitch, and its dust into brimstone;

Its land shall become burning pitch. ¹⁰ It shall not be quenched night or day; Its smoke shall ascend forever. From generation to generation, it shall lie waste; No one shall pass through it forever and ever." **Isaiah 34:5-10**

"⁷ Against Edom. Thus says the LORD of hosts: "Is wisdom no more in Teman? Has counsel perished from the prudent? Has their wisdom vanished? ⁸ Flee, turn back, dwell in the depths, O inhabitants of Dedan! For I will bring the calamity of Esau upon him, the time that I will punish him. ⁹ If grape-gatherers came to you, would they not leave some gleaning grapes? If thieves by night, would they not destroy until they have enough? ¹⁰ But I have made Esau bare; I have uncovered his secret places, and he shall not be able to hide himself. His descendants are plundered, His brethren and his neighbors, and he is no more. ¹¹ Leave your fatherless children, I will preserve them alive; and let your widows trust in Me." **Jeremiah 49:7-11**

"²¹ Rejoice and be glad, O daughter of Edom, you who dwell in the land of Uz! The cup shall also pass over to you, and you shall become drunk and make yourself naked. ²² The punishment of your iniquity is accomplished, O daughter of Zion; He will no longer send you into captivity. He will punish your iniquity, O daughter of Edom; He will uncover your sins!" **Lamentations 4:21-22**

"¹² 'Thus says the Lord GOD: "Because of what Edom did against the house of Judah by taking vengeance, and has greatly offended by avenging itself on them," ¹³ therefore thus says the Lord GOD: "I will also stretch out My hand against Edom, cut off man and beast from it, and make it desolate from Teman; Dedan shall fall by the sword. ¹⁴ I will lay My vengeance on Edom by the hand of My people Israel, that they may do in Edom according to My anger and according to My fury; and they shall know My vengeance," says the Lord GOD." **Ezekiel 25:12-14**

There are similar pronouncements concerning Edom in Joel 3:19, Amos 1:11-12; 9:11-12, and Malachi 1:4.

So, why did the Most High God say he hated Esau and his descendants, the Edomites?

Well, it all began with Esau and Jacob, Isaac's twin sons, in the womb of their mother, Rebekah. The children were fighting within her womb, yes fighting, and she inquired of the Lord what was happening with the children.

"[21] Isaac prayed to the LORD on behalf of his wife, because she was childless. The LORD answered his prayer, and his wife Rebekah became pregnant. [22]The babies jostled each other within her, and she said, "Why is this happening to me?" **So, she went to inquire of the LORD.** [23]**The LORD said to her,** "Two nations are in your womb, and two peoples from within you will be separated, one people will be stronger than the other, and **the older will serve the younger.""** **Gen.25:21-23**

Now, let us examine the Lord's response, "Two nations." We know that this speaks of Israel (Jacob) and Edom (Esau). These two nations will contain "two manners of people," godless (Esau) and God-fearing (Jacob), fleshly minded (Esau) and spiritually minded (Jacob), earth dweller (Esau), and kingdom guest (Jacob).

When we probe the personalities of Isaac's two sons, Esau minded earthly possessions, while Jacob minded heavenly possessions.

What is of great importance to note is that God's election of Jacob over Esau was done prior to their birth.

"⁶ It is not as though God's word had failed. For not all who are descended from Israel are Israel. ⁷ Nor because they are his descendants are they all Abraham's children. On the contrary, "It is through Isaac that your offspring will be reckoned." ⁸ In other words, it is not the children by physical descent who are God's children, but it is the children of the promise who are regarded as Abraham's offspring. ⁹ For this was how the promise was stated: "At the appointed time I will return, and Sarah will have a son." ¹⁰ Not only that, but Rebekah's children were conceived at the same time by our father Isaac. ¹¹ Yet, before the twins were born or had done anything good or bad —in order that God's purpose in election might stand: ¹² not by works but by him who calls—she was told, "The older will serve the younger." ¹³ Just as it is written: "Jacob I loved, but Esau I hated." **Romans 9:6-13**

You ask: Why God?

First and foremost, because it was in God's heart to select Jacob, furthermore, He also knew their future. This is not dissimilar to the election God made between Ishmael and Isaac, Abraham's sons. The Lord once spoke to Abraham concerning Isaac, take him to Mount Mariah and sacrifice him to Me. Now do not get the wrong impression of the Lord. He is not condoning human sacrifice, which is an abomination unto Him. What God was doing was testing Abraham's faithfulness, not to prove it to God, who knows all things, past, present, and future, but to Abraham. Remember, Abraham had previously gone through nine tests, some he failed and had to repeat while others he passed, and his faith was strengthened.

One of the failed tests was when he left the Promised Land during a famine and journeyed into Egypt instead of trusting the Lord to be his provider. This resulted in Abraham's wife, Sarah, receiving an Egyptian slave-girl named Hagar. Since she was barren and nearly past the age of childbearing, Sarah convinced Abraham to have relations with her maidservant Hagar to bear a child. Abraham complied, and Hagar conceived. When Hagar conceived, she despised Sarah for being barren, which infuriated Sarah. Sarah discussed the situation with Abraham, who said to her, Hagar is your maidservant, do with her as you please. Sarah then began to deal harshly with Hagar, so intensely that she fled for her life while pregnant with child. The Lord then sought out Hagar and commanded her to go back to Sarah. He would protect her from harm, then gave her a promise of an abundance of descendants. Then the Lord told Hagar that she will have a son whom God named Ishmael. Yes, God spoke directly to Hagar, who was a slave, and named her child.

" [7] Now the Angel of the LORD found her by a spring of water in the wilderness, by the spring on the way to Shur. [8] And He said, "Hagar, Sarai's maid, where have you come from, and where are you going?" She said, "I am fleeing from the presence of my mistress Sarai." [9] The Angel of the LORD said to her, "Return to your mistress, and submit yourself under her hand." [10] Then the Angel of the LORD said to her, "I will multiply your descendants exceedingly, so that they shall not be counted for multitude." [11] And the Angel of the LORD said to her: "Behold, you are with child, And you shall bear a son. You shall call his name Ishmael because the LORD has heard your affliction. [12] He shall be a wild man; his hand shall be against every man, and every man's hand against him. And he shall dwell in the presence of all his brethren."" **Genesis 16:7-12**

CHAPTER 2

THE SON OF PROMISE

Abraham was 86 years old when Ishmael was born. Fourteen years later, Sarah gave birth to Isaac, yet the Lord told Abraham that Isaac was his only son.

Why did the Lord say that?

Because Isaac was the only son of promise and a type of Christ by being born miraculously. Both Abraham and Sarah were beyond the years of childbearing. Therefore, Sarah could not become pregnant by natural causes. It had to be a miracle performed by God.

"⁹ Then they said to him, "Where is Sarah your wife?" So he said, "Here, in the tent."¹⁰ And He said, "I will certainly return to you according to the time of life, and behold, Sarah your wife shall have a son." (Sarah was listening in the tent door which was behind him.) ¹¹ Now Abraham and Sarah were old, well advanced in age, and Sarah had passed the age of childbearing.¹² Therefore Sarah laughed within herself, saying, "After I have grown old, shall I have pleasure, my lord being old also?"¹³ And the LORD said to Abraham, "Why did Sarah laugh, saying, 'Shall I surely bear a child, since I am old?'¹⁴ Is anything too hard for the LORD? At the appointed time I will return to you, according to the time of life, and Sarah shall have a son." **Genesis 18:9-14**

I stated above concerning Isaac that he was a type of Christ by way of a miraculous birth. Christ the Lord was born of a virgin, which definitely qualifies as a miracle. Likewise, Isaac was in his thirties when God commanded Abraham to journey to Mount Moriah to sacrifice Isaac to God upon an altar. With Abraham being 100 years old when Isaac was born, this event took place approximately 33 years later. There was no way that Abraham could have bonded Isaac with rope unless Isaac volunteered to go along with the plan. We see the same thing with the Lord Jesus, who was 33 years old when he willingly gave up his life that we may live.

"[2] Then God said, "**Take your son, your only son**, whom you love Isaac and go to the region of Moriah. Sacrifice him there as a burnt offering on a mountain I will show you."...[12] "Do not lay a hand on the boy," he said. "Do not do anything to him. Now I know that you fear God, because you have not withheld from me **your son, your only son**."...[16] and said, "I swear by myself, declares the LORD, that because you have done this and have not withheld **your son, your only son**," **Genesis 22:2, 12, 16**

Abraham passed his final exam with a perfect score, placing his faith in God's ability to raise Isaac from the dead. Having time to reflect on God's command (God does not make a request) during the three-day journey, Abraham had plenty of time to reflect upon God's command. Nevertheless, he did not waver having complete confidence in the Lord. Upon arrival at Mount Moriah, he spoke this to his two servants.

"⁵ And Abraham said to his young men, "Stay here with the donkey; the lad and I will go yonder and worship, and we will come back to you." **Genesis 22:5**

Notice that Abraham stated, "**we** will come back to you." Oh beloved, if we all could have faith and trust in the Lord like Abraham did, as he matured in his walk with God.

* * *

What a heritage to pass on to his son, Isaac. Abraham witnessed his lifestyle to his family, and Isaac, who saw it firsthand and matured in faith toward the Lord like his father.

It is evident that Isaac taught both of his sons how to seek and serve God. We see Jacob building altars. However, Esau had no respect for spiritual things. According to the word of God, Esau despised his birthright, being the firstborn of his father, Isaac.

"²⁹ Now Jacob cooked a stew; and Esau came in from the field, and he was weary. ³⁰ And Esau said to Jacob, "Please feed me with that same red stew, for I am weary." Therefore, his name was called Edom. ³¹ But Jacob said, "Sell me your birthright as of this day." ³² And Esau said, "Look, I am about to die; so, what is this birthright to me?" ³³ Then Jacob said, "Swear to me as of this day." So, he swore to him, and sold his birthright to Jacob. ³⁴ And Jacob gave Esau bread and stew of lentils; then he ate and drank, arose, and went his way. Thus, Esau despised his birthright." **Genesis 25:29-34**

You may ask: Why does Esau despising being the firstborn matter?

Because it mattered to God. The firstborn represented Jesus Christ, who is the first begotten of the Father. The Father declared this truth through the prophet, King David, in the Psalms.

"¹ I will declare the decree; the Lord hath said unto me, ²Thou art my Son, **this day have I begotten thee**. (speaking of the resurrection)" **Psalms 27:1-2**

In **Psalms 89:23-29** God declared; that David's "horn (speaking of Christ) shall be exalted...He (Christ) shall cry unto me, Thou art my father, my God, and the rock of my salvation (speaking of the cross)...Also I will make him (Christ) **my firstborn** (speaking of the resurrection)...higher than the kings of the earth...His seed (Christ) also shall I make to endure forever, and his (Christ's) throne as the days of heaven."

God told Moses that all the firstborn of Israel are mine, then traded their rights for the tribe of Levi, to do the priestly service unto Him in the tabernacle and future temples. This was done because of the rebellious nature of the Jewish people as they journeyed to the Promised Land after the Lord delivered them from Egyptian bondage. It was the plan of God to have the entire nation be priests, yet they fell into apostasy. Nevertheless, it will be fulfilled in the future Millennium Kingdom of the Lord Jesus. On that day, all Israel will be saved and made priests before the Lord. A light on a hill shinning in a dark and evil world, leading people to the Savior.

Num. 3:10-13 The LORD said to Moses, "Bring the tribe of Levi and present them to Aaron the priest to assist him. ⁷ They are to perform duties for him and for the whole community at the tent of meeting by doing the work of the tabernacle. ⁸ They are to take care of all the furnishings of the tent of meeting, fulfilling the obligations of the Israelites by doing the work of the tabernacle. ⁹ Give the Levites to Aaron and his sons; they are the Israelites who are to be given wholly to him. ¹⁰ Appoint Aaron and his sons to serve as priests; anyone else who approaches the sanctuary is to be put to death." [11] The LORD also said to Moses, [12] **"I have taken the Levites from among the Israelites in place of the first male offspring of every Israelite woman. The Levites are mine,** [13] **for all the firstborn are mine**. When I struck down all the firstborn in Egypt, **I set apart for myself every firstborn in Israel, whether human or animal. They are to be mine. I am the LORD."**

In **Col. 1:15-17** we read, "He is the image of the invisible God, **the firstborn (creator) over all creation.** [16] For by Him all things were created that are in heaven and that are on earth, visible and invisible, whether thrones or dominions or principalities or powers. All things were created through Him and for Him. [17] And He is before all things, and in Him all things consist."

In **Col. 1:18** speaking of the resurrection we read, "and He is the head of the body, the church, who is the beginning, **the firstborn from the dead** that in all things He may have the preeminence."

In **Heb. 12:22-23** it is said that we did not arrive at "Mt. Sinai but to the New Jerusalem…to the general assembly and church of **the firstborn…"**

All of God lives in Jesus Christ. This was spoken by Paul to the Church at Colosse to combat the heresy and the conveyance of divine powers, and God attributes to multiple emanations. Paul countered these false doctrines by asserting that the fullness of the Godhead (deity), inclusive of all divine powers, attributes, and dominion, was not divided among created entities but completely resident in Jesus Christ alone.

"[19] For it pleased the Father that in Him all the fullness should dwell, [20] and by Him to reconcile all things to Himself, by Him, whether things on earth or things in heaven, having made peace through the blood of His cross." **Colossians 1:19-20**

Jesus is the only begotten Son of the Father. Adam was a son of God, but Jesus is the Son of God.

"[14] The Word became flesh and made his dwelling among us. We have seen his glory, the glory of the one and only Son, who came from the Father, full of grace and truth. [15] (John testified concerning him. He cried out, saying, "This is the one I spoke about when I said, 'He who comes after me has surpassed me because he was before me.'") [16] Out of his fullness we have all received grace in place of grace already given. [17] For the law was given through Moses; grace and truth came through Jesus Christ. [18] No one has ever seen God, but the one and only Son, who is himself God and is in closest relationship with the Father, has made him known." **John 1:14-18**

Do you now understand the importance and value that God places on the firstborn? The firstborn was to inherit all things or a double portion if there were more than one sibling. Since Jesus alone is the Son of God, he inherited all things.

"[18] Jesus came and spake unto them, saying, all power is given unto me, in heaven and in earth." **Mat. 28:18**

"[7] In him we have redemption through his blood, the forgiveness of sins, in accordance with the riches of God's grace [8] that he lavished on us. With all wisdom and understanding, [9] he made known to us the mystery of his will according to his good pleasure, which he purposed in Christ, [10] to be put into effect when the times reach their fulfillment **to bring unity to all things in heaven and on earth under Christ**." **Ephesians 1:7-10**

Beloved, this is what Esau despised and Jacob embraced.

You say: How do you know that?

Well, we can examine their lives as presented in the scriptures. Esau's descendants were all pagan idol worshipers, and it was Esau's descendants who attempted to kill the Lord Jesus at his birth! Herod the Great was an Edomite who ordered the slaughter of thousands of Jewish babies up to age two when he determined that the magi (Wise Men) deceived him. Let's take just a brief detour to develop how this came to be.

CHAPTER 3

HISTORICAL VIEW–DESCENDANTS OF ESAU. WHO WAS HEROD?

It happens every Christmas season; certain characters always come to mind, such as the angel Gabriel, the only angel to speak on behalf of God in the Bible. It was Gabriel who announced to Zacharias while he was serving in the temple, presenting the offering of incense unto the Lord. Gabriel told Zacharias that his wife Elizabeth, who had been barren and beyond the age of childbearing, would bear a son. Does that sound familiar? Of course, Zacharias thought more about he and Elizabeth's age than the fact an angel from God was speaking to him. Therefore, he doubted the words of the Lord. For his unbelief, the Lord made him mute until the child was born.

This son was to be named John; God named him too. We know him as John the Baptist. The prophets Isaiah and Malachi prophesied concerning John the Baptist,

"³ The voice of one crying in the wilderness: "Prepare the way of the LORD; Make straight in the desert A highway for our God."
Isaiah 40:3

"¹ "Behold, I send My messenger, and he will prepare the way before Me. And the Lord, whom you seek, Will suddenly come to His temple, Even the Messenger of the covenant, in whom you delight. Behold, He is coming," says the LORD of hosts." **Malachi 3:1**

Then we have Mary, to whom the angel Gabriel was also sent by the Lord. Gabriel told Mary that she would bear the Messiah, the Son of God, the Savior of the world. Mary also questioned Gabriel concerning this pronouncement, and Gabriel explained to her in like manner as with Zacharias. However, Mary believed the Lord's words and submitted herself as a bondservant to His will.

"³⁴ Then Mary said to the angel, "How can this be, since I do not know a man?" ³⁵ And the angel answered and said to her, "The Holy Spirit will come upon you, and the power of the Highest will overshadow you; therefore, also, that Holy One who is to be born will be called the Son of God... ³⁸ Then Mary said, "Behold the maidservant of the Lord! Let it be to me according to your word." And the angel departed from her."" **Luke 1:34-35, 38**

Next on our Christmas parade was Mary's husband, Joseph, who was an honorable man. As time passed and it became known that Mary was with child, the whispers began. One must understand Jewish customs during those days, as it was forbidden for espoused couples to consummate the marriage until after the wedding ceremony. Even though espoused couples were legally married in the eyes of Jewish law, the customs of that day were religiously enforced. Obviously, knowing that he and Mary had not consummated the marriage, Joseph was deeply wounded and troubled. How could the woman I love be unfaithful to our vows even before our wedding day? Therefore, he sought privately to divorce Mary due to her supposed unfaithfulness.

The Lord himself intervened to keep Joseph from divorcing Mary by speaking to Joseph in a dream concerning his wife's pregnancy.

"[19] Then Joseph her husband, being a just man, and not wanting to make her a public example, was minded to put her away secretly. [20] But while he thought about these things, behold, an angel of the Lord appeared to him in a dream, saying, "Joseph, son of David, do not be afraid to take to you Mary your wife, for that which is conceived in her is of the Holy Spirit. [21] And she will bring forth a Son, and you shall call His name JESUS, for He will save His people from their sins."" **Matthew 1:19-21**

Oh, by the way, God named him too.

Then there is always the mention of the decree of Caesar Augustus, who unwittingly assisted with the fulfillment of the prophecy having the Lord Jesus being born in Bethlehem due to his greed for taxes. He literally taxed the whole world! What a greedy rascal.

"[1] And it came to pass in those days that a decree went out from Caesar Augustus that all the world should be registered." **Luke 2:1**

We cannot leave out the shepherds in the field tending their sheep as a chorus of angels announced the birth of the Savior, Christ the Lord, and sang praises to His glorious name.

"[8] Now there were in the same country shepherds living out in the fields, keeping watch over their flock by night. [9] And behold, an angel of the Lord stood before them, and the glory of the

Lord shone around them, and they were greatly afraid. [10] Then the angel said to them, "Do not be afraid, for behold, I bring you good tidings of great joy which will be to all people. [11] For there is born to you this day in the city of David a Savior, who is Christ the Lord. [12] And this will be the sign to you: You will find a Babe wrapped in swaddling cloths, lying in a manger." [13] And suddenly there was with the angel a multitude of the heavenly host praising God and saying: [14] "Glory to God in the highest, And on earth peace, goodwill toward men!"'" **Luke 2:8-14**

We are still awaiting the fulfillment of the last half of verse 14. There will be no peace on earth until the Prince of Peace, the Lord Jesus Christ, returns.

Finally, there were the Wise Men from the east who were observing the times even though the rulers of the Jews were not. They came to a man who considered himself the king of the Jews and sought to know where this One who was born the true King of the Jews was laid.

"[1] Now after Jesus was born in Bethlehem of Judea in the days of Herod the king, behold, wise men from the east came to Jerusalem, [2] saying, "Where is He who has been born King of the Jews? For we have seen His star in the east and have come to worship Him."'" **Matthew 2:1-2**

The Bible records that when Herod, the king of Judea, heard their words, he was troubled and all Jerusalem with him.

Why would Jerusalem be trouble with Herod?

This was primarily speaking of the Jewish leaders. Herod was troubled because there was another who was not his heir making claims to be the King of the Jews. One would have to know a little regarding Herod's family history to fully understand that statement. His family was a group of psychopathic murderers, and he was chief among them.

"³ When Herod the king heard this, he was troubled, and all Jerusalem with him. ⁴ And when he had gathered all the chief priests and scribes of the people together, he inquired of them where the Christ was to be born.'"" **Matthew 2:3-4**

During Jesus' time on earth, Herod and his sons ruled all Judea, and they were hostile toward anyone who challenged their rights to the throne, and I mean anyone including members of the royal family. Of course, that didn't extend to Caesar as Judea was a Roman province. The Roman emperor assigned Herod the Great to the throne in the Judean province as he declared that the Edomites and Jews were of the same family. It is not certain if he actually knew that to be true; nevertheless, that's what he declared. Let us then briefly examine the Herod family tree.

King Herod 1 (The Great). The name Herod was the name of various members of the royal dynasty, which originated in Edom (Edom is Esau), which the Romans and Greeks before them called Idumea. They were conquered by the Jews in the Maccabean revolution led by the Hammer, John Hyrcanus, the son of the Simon Maccabeus, the son of Mattathias Maccabeus, the son of Judas Maccabeus who led the rebellion against the Syrian tyrant, Antiochus IV Epiphanes. Yes, that Antiochus Epiphanes who desecrated the Temple of the Lord by setting up an altar to Zeus over the altar of burnt offerings and offering a pig on the altar committing the abomination of desecration spoken of by Daniel the prophet.

"²⁹ "At the appointed time, he shall return and go toward the south; but it shall not be like the former or the latter. ³⁰ For ships from Cyprus shall come against him; therefore he shall be grieved, and return in rage against the holy covenant, and do damage. "So he shall return and show regard for those who forsake the holy covenant. ³¹ And forces shall be mustered by him, and they shall defile the sanctuary fortress; then they shall take away the daily sacrifices, and place there the abomination of desolation. ³² Those who do wickedly against the covenant he shall corrupt with flattery; but the people who know their God shall be strong, and carry out great exploits." **Daniel 11:29-32**

Herod the Great was the son of Antipater and was made king by Rome in 40 BC. Under his rule were the areas of Judea Samaria, Galilee, Idumea (Edom), Batanea, and Peracea, which were equivalent to the areas ruled by David and Solomon, Kings of Israel. Herod the Great was a madman, and although he married a Jew, his insolence and cruelty knew no mercy. Anyone he thought was a threat was immediately executed.

Herod's constant fear of conspiracy and outrageous brutality caused many of the Jews to dislike him. Herod executed his wife when he suspected she was plotting against him—not that she really was plotting against him. Three of his sons, another wife, and his mother-in-law met the same fate when they too were suspected of a coup conspiracy. This man killed his brother-in-law, several other wives, and almost all his sons. He had many children, but I can't understand why.

Even with all his madman antics, Herod was a master builder, and his policy of Hellenistic culture truly angered the Jews he ruled. Herod constructed racecourses, theaters, a great amphitheater along with several pagan temples. Yet, he curried favor with the Jewish leaders when he reconstructed the Temple of the Lord. This was the temple that Jesus visited.

Though the Jewish rulers remained in favor with Herod, the Jewish people hated that an Edomite was ruling over their land. Herod the Great also massacred the children of Bethlehem, two years old and younger, in his rage to murder the Messiah, the true King of the Jews. True to his nature, when he became sick unto death, Herod imprisoned all the Jewish leaders and commanded that they should be executed at his death.

You ask: Why?

Herod's reasoning was since no one would mourn over the loss of his presence, at least there would be mourning in the city to make pretense that it was for him.

After Herod the Great's death in 4 BC, his remaining three sons each declared their accession to the throne. Due to the conflict, Caesar Augustus divided the kingdom among them. Archelaus, the elder son, was given Judea with the promise to be named king if he ruled well, but he failed and was removed by Caesar. His area was then given to Roman governors, with Pontius Pilate being assigned during the days of Jesus. Other governors mentioned in the Bible were Felix and Festus, before whom Paul stood trial.

Herod Antipas was named tetrarch of Galilee and Perea by Caesar. He ruled this area during Jesus' public ministry. This is the Herod who beheaded John the Baptist for speaking out against his marriage to Herodias, his brother Philip's ex-wife. This is also the Herod who threatened Jesus' life and who the Lord called "that fox." Herod finally got his wish to meet Jesus when He stood before Pilate at the trial, hoping that Jesus would perform some miracle in his presence.

Herod's other son, Philip, became tetrarch of Iturea, Trachonitis, Gaulanitis, Auranitis, and Batanea, which were the areas north and east of Galilee. Philip died without an heir.

The only other Herod descendants mentioned in the scriptures were Herod the Great's grandson, Herod Agrippa I, and great-grandson Herod Agrippa II. It was Herod Agrippa I who hunted down James and Peter. Shortly after their arrest, James was executed. However, Peter escaped death by the Lord sending an angel to lead him out of the dungeon. Herod Agrippa 1 was struck down by God for attempting to make himself a god, thereby attempting to take glory from the One true God.

"[18] Then, as soon as it was day, there was no small stir among the soldiers about what had become of Peter. [19] But when Herod had searched for him and not found him, he examined the guards and commanded that they should be put to death. And he went down from Judea to Caesarea, and stayed there. [20] Now Herod had been very angry with the people of Tyre and Sidon; but they came to him with one accord, and having made Blastus the king's personal aide their friend, they asked for peace, because their country was supplied with food by the king's country. [21] So on a set day Herod, arrayed in royal apparel, sat on his throne and gave an oration to them. [22] And the people kept shouting, "The voice of a god and not of a man!" [23] Then immediately an angel of the Lord struck him, because he did not give glory to God. And he was eaten by worms and died. [24] But the word of God grew and multiplied.""
Acts 12:18-24

Herod Agrippa II ascended to the throne after the death of his father. It was this Herod who joined Roman governor Festus at Paul's trial.

"²⁸ Then Agrippa said to Paul, "You almost persuade me to become a Christian." ²⁹ And Paul said, "I would to God that not only you, but also all who hear me today, might become both almost and altogether such as I am, except for these chains." **Acts 26:28-29**

From the accounts above, we can now see how the descendants of Esau interacted with the descendants of Jacob and how cruelly they treated the Jewish people. The Edomites attempted several times to kill the Messiah or his lineage to prevent His birth. Esau, who is Edom, despised his birthright, married two Canaanite women that God had forbidden him to marry, then attempted to annihilate the lineage of Christ. What a sad and awful scene.

CHAPTER 4

ESAU's LITTLE SECRET

You may think: Well, how would God know the history of Esau's lineage?

My friend, God knows every possible choice we can make and the results (impact) of each possible choice before we select one. He takes that decision we make and ultimately uses it to accomplish His own will. It's like a 12-spoke wheel with the hub being the perfect will of God and our decisions being the spokes, yet everything is still dependent upon the foundational hub (the centerline). The rim and hub are the providential will of God (like the back office in computer software language), which is the government of the physical realm in which we live. The governing laws are things like gravity, the laws of thermodynamics, sowing, and reaping, etc., in the physical universe. Then you have God's sovereignty, decrees, immutable counsel, etc., in the spiritual universe. These governing laws can be discovered as some already have, yet none can be broken, but that's a topic for another day.

It is no wonder God declared, "Jacob I have loved, and Esau have I hated." **Rom. 9:13**

We get a further explanation in **Heb. 12:16-17,** which declares, "Let's there be any fornicator (immoral), or profane person (godless, idol worshipper), **as Esau**, who for one morsel of meat sold his birthright."

God dedicated an entire Old Testament book to plead his case against Esau, who is Edom. In the book of Obadiah, we read, "Thus saith the Lord concerning Edom...." **Obadiah 1:1**

Now, beloved, that is direct. There's no guessing about whom the Lord is referring.

"² "Behold, I will make you small among the nations; you shall be greatly despised." **Obadiah 1:2**

Edom had exalted himself, enlarged his britches, and magnified himself in his own eyes.

You ask: By whom was Edom despised?

Well, by the Lord God.

This is just the opposite of what God spoke concerning Israel, "⁹ For the Lord's portion is his people, Jacob is the lot of his inheritance. ¹⁰He found him in a desert land, and in a waste howling wilderness; he led him about, he instructed him, he kept him as the apple of his eye." **Deut. 23:9-10**

"⁴ For the Lord has chosen Jacob unto himself, and Israel for his peculiar treasure." **Ps. 135:4**

Why would the Lord greatly despise Esau and Edom?

"³ The pride of thine heart hath deceived thee, thou that dwellest in the clefts of the rock, whose habitation is high; that saith in his heart, who can bring me down to the ground?" **Obad. 1:3**

It was pride! The same sin that brought down Lucifer, who is Satan, who led the rebellion in heaven and has wreaked havoc upon the earth. He tempted Eve and deceived her into sinning against the Lord, which led to Adam's overt sin and the fall of mankind with him. This wicked one will be responsible for billions of people being cast into the lake of fire.

Listen to the Lord's description of the fall of the first rebel, Satan, and how he was judged.

"[12] How art thou fallen from heaven, O Lucifer, son of the morning! How art thou cut down to the ground, which didst weaken the nations! [13] For thou hast said in thine heart, I will ascend into heaven, I will exalt my throne above the stars of God: I will sit also upon the mount of the congregation, in the sides of the north: [14] I will ascend above the heights of the clouds; I will be like the Most High. [15] Yet thou shalt be brought down to hell, to the sides of the pit. [16] They that see thee shall narrowly look upon thee, and consider thee, saying, Is this the man that made the earth to tremble, that did shake kingdoms; [17] That made the world as a wilderness, and destroyed the cities thereof; that opened not the house of his prisoners? [18] All the kings of the nations, even all of them, lie in glory, every one in his own house. [19] But thou art cast out of thy grave like an abominable branch, and as the raiment of those that are slain, thrust through with a sword, that go down to the stones of the pit; as a carcase trodden under feet. [20] Thou shalt not be joined with them in burial, because thou hast destroyed thy land, and slain thy people: the seed of evildoers shall never be renowned." **Isaiah 14:12-20**

Although Satan is the most powerful creator God has ever created, he does not come close to matching the Lord in power, wisdom, and might. As a matter of fact, the Lord God is infinitely more powerful than all His creation together.

Next, we had Cain, who killed his brother, Able, because he chose to rebel against the commandment of the Lord by bringing an offering without blood, the works of his own hands, to a holy God. As if his rebellion would be overlooked.

Then Pharaoh would not allow God's people, Israel, to depart Egypt believing he could withstand the hand of God. Pharaoh also gave orders to kill every male child born to the Hebrews when they were slaves in Egypt in another attempt by Satan to stop the birth of Christ by eliminating the Jews.

Then there was Sennacherib, king of Assyria, who wrote a letter to Hezekiah mocking the Lord of Glory, saying, "and who is that God who can deliver Judah out of my hand." What a fool! The Lord sent the death angel that night who killed 185,000 Assyrian soldiers in one night, leaving Sennacherib to travel back to his country alone. He found out that there truly is a God in Israel. But it wasn't over for ole Sennacherib. Upon his return to the palace, two of his sons assassinated him.

We cannot forget about Herod, the pervert who married his brother's ex-wife and lusted so deeply after his niece that one provocative dance caused the madman to behead John the Baptist. This wicked man also attempted to kill the Lord when He was a baby, slaughtering thousands of babies in Bethlehem. He died miserable and alone.

Finally, there will be the Beast, better known as the antichrist. He will be the epitome of evil, possessed personally by the devil who will give the Beast all the authority he took from Adam. The Beast will murder hundreds of millions of Christians and Jews in his bloodlust to stop the fulfillment of the plan of God, sending Jesus Christ, His Son, back to the earth to rule over it from the throne of David in Jerusalem. In the end, just like the others, the antichrist fails, and he will be the first occupant in the lake of fire. He and his partner in wickedness, the false prophet, will be cast into the lake of fire while they are still alive.

The word of God declares that "[18] Pride goes before destruction and a haughty spirit before a fall." **Prov. 16:18**

What caused Esau to be so prideful? "[4] Though you soar like the eagle and make your nest among the stars, from there I will bring you down," declares the LORD." **Obad. 1:4**

Esau's pride was that he did not need God, that he would do things his own way, that he could come to God without the blood sacrifice as instructed but with the works of his hands. Just like Cain, Edom exalted himself like the eagle. The eagle represents deity; Edom made himself equal to God. Just like Satan said in his heart, Esau would nest among the stars and be like the Most High! Yet God proclaimed, just as He said about the devil, that He will cast Esau down to the ground. That He will severely judge Edom.

You may be thinking: How did Edom make himself equal to God?

Anytime anyone says in their heart that I will come to God my own way and not the way God has commanded, that person is implying they are equal in power and authority with God. And by your power, God must accept your terms. Of course, that will never be true.

The Babylonian king, Nebuchadnezzar, who conquered the known world of his day, had something to say to himself, not understanding that he was challenging God. He was full of himself, marveling at the power of his own might and glory, not understanding how fleeting it was.

"³⁰ The king spoke, saying, "Is not this great Babylon, that I have built for a royal dwelling by my mighty power and for the honor of my majesty?" **Daniel 4:30**

For those words, the Lord made the boastful king of the world eat grass like a cow for seven years. Afterward, he came to his senses.

"³⁴ "At the end of that time, I, Nebuchadnezzar, raised my eyes toward heaven, and my sanity was restored. Then I praised the Most High; I honored and glorified him who lives forever. His dominion is an eternal dominion; his kingdom endures from generation to generation. ³⁵ **All the peoples of the earth are regarded as nothing. He does as he pleases with the powers of heaven and the peoples of the earth. No one can hold back his hand or say to him: "What have you done?"** Daniel 4:34-35

Well, Edom had a secret. Now it has been said that hidden sins on earth are open scandal in heaven.

"⁶ How are the things of Esau searched out! How are his hidden things sought up!" **Obad. 1:6**

What were Edom's hidden things?

To discover that, we must travel back in time. God commanded the Israelites that they were not to hate their relatives, the Edomites.

"⁷ Do not despise an Edomite, for the Edomites are related to you. Do not despise an Egyptian, because you resided as foreigners in their country." **Deut. 23:7**

Nevertheless, we read in **Num. 20:14-21** that Moses asked Edom to pass through their land on the way to the Holy Land, and Edom refused.

"[14] Moses sent messengers from Kadesh to the king of Edom, saying: "This is what your brother Israel says: You know about all the hardships that have come on us. [15] Our ancestors went down into Egypt, and we lived there many years. The Egyptians mistreated us and our ancestors, [16] but when we cried out to the LORD, he heard our cry and sent an angel and brought us out of Egypt. "Now we are here at Kadesh, a town on the edge of your territory. [17] Please let us pass through your country. We will not go through any field or vineyard, or drink water from any well. We will travel along the King's Highway and not turn to the right or to the left until we have passed through your territory." [18] But Edom answered: "You may not pass through here; if you try, we will march out and attack you with the sword." [19] The Israelites replied: "We will go along the main road, and if we or our livestock drink any of your water, we will pay for it. We only want to pass through on foot, nothing else." [20] Again they answered: "You may not pass through." Then Edom came out against them with a large and powerful army. [21] Since Edom refused to let them go through their territory, Israel turned away from them." **Numbers 20:14-21**

You may say: Is that all? Edom was only attempting to protect his border.

No, beloved, he was not. Let me remind you again of what the Lord said, "How are the things of Esau searched out! How are the hidden things sought up!" Now let me show you what Edom did to Israel on that day.

"¹¹ Thus says the LORD: "For three transgressions of Edom, and for four, I will not turn away its punishment, because he pursued his brother with the sword, and cast off all pity; His anger tore perpetually, and he kept his wrath forever. ¹² But I will send a fire upon Teman, Which shall devour the palaces of Bozrah."
Amos 1:11-12

The devil used Edom to make the children of Israel take the long route to the Promised Land in the hope that they would die during the journey. It was the devil's failed attempt again to thwart the plan of God and keep the Lord from fulfilling his promise to Abraham, thereby keeping the Messiah from being born. It was always in his heart to kill the children of Israel through whom the Messiah would come. What did Esau say in his heart after forfeiting his birthright to Jacob?

"⁴¹ Esau held a grudge against Jacob because of the blessing his father had given him. He said to himself, "The days of mourning for my father are near; **then I will kill my brother Jacob.**"
Genesis 27:41

Does not that remind you of Cain? Esau was a murderer. In his heart and mind, Jacob was already dead. Jacob represented the promised seed through whom the Messiah would be born. If Jacob was killed, Satan could claim victory over the Lord because He would have failed to keep His promise to Abraham and Isaac.

Ever since conception, his descendants, the earth dwellers, the Edomites or Idumeans as they later became called by the Greeks and Romans, became the arch enemies of Israel and the King of Israel, the Lord of hosts. Esau was full of pride. Thinking himself to be wise, he became a fool.

"¹² "I, wisdom, dwell with prudence, and find out knowledge and discretion. ¹³ The fear of the LORD is to hate evil; Pride and arrogance and the evil way and the perverse mouth I hate." **Proverbs 8:12-13**

CHAPTER 5

A REBEL AT HEART

Before and after not obtaining the blessing of the firstborn, in a blatant act of open rebellion against his parents, Esau intermarried with the Canaanites, with whom he was forbidden to marry.

"¹ Abraham was now very old, and the LORD had blessed him in every way. ² He said to the senior servant in his household, the one in charge of all that he had, "Put your hand under my thigh. ³ I want you to swear by the LORD, the God of heaven and the God of earth, that **you will not get a wife for my son from the daughters of the Canaanites**, among whom I am living, ⁴ but will go to my country and my own relatives and get a wife for my son Isaac." **Genesis 24:1-4**

"¹ So Isaac called for Jacob and blessed him. Then he commanded him: "**Do not marry a Canaanite woman.** ² Go at once to Paddan Aram, to the house of your mother's father Bethuel. Take a wife for yourself there, from among the daughters of Laban, your mother's brother. ³ May God Almighty bless you and make you fruitful and increase your numbers until you become a community of peoples. ⁴ May he give you and your descendants the blessing given to Abraham, so that you may take possession of the land where you now reside as a foreigner, the land God gave to Abraham." ⁵ Then Isaac sent Jacob on his way, and he went to Paddan Aram, to Laban son of Bethuel the Aramean, the brother of Rebekah, who was the mother of Jacob and Esau." **Genesis 28:1-5**

"³⁴ When Esau was forty years old, he married Judith daughter of Beeri the Hittite, and also Basemath daughter of Elon the Hittite. ³⁵**They were a source of grief to Isaac and Rebekah**." **Genesis 26:34-35**

Esau never consulted Isaac, which was the custom because the son's wife would be brought into the father's house. This is no small oversight as this speaks of Christ and his bride, the Church. Notice that Abraham selects Isaac's wife, and Isaac selects Jacob's wife. Likewise, God the Father has selected the Church to be his Son, Jesus' wife.

"³⁷ All those **the Father gives me will come to me**, and whoever comes to me I will never drive away…No one can come to me unless **the Father who sent me draws them**, and I will raise them up at the last day" **John 6:37-38, 44**

"¹ Father, the hour has come. Glorify your Son, that your Son may glorify you. ²For you granted him authority over all people **that he might give eternal life to all those you have given Him**. ³Now this is eternal life: that they know you, the only true God, and Jesus Christ, whom you have sent." **John 17:1-3**

Oh, beloved, please do not miss this great truth; the Church is the love gift from the Father to the Son! Eternal life is a person, Jesus Christ.

"¹¹ And this is the testimony: God has given us eternal life, and **this life is in His Son**. ¹² Whoever has the Son has life; whoever does not have the Son of God does not have life." **1 John 5:11-12**

If the Spirit of Christ is living inside of you, you have eternal life and are headed for heaven after physical death. If the Spirit of Christ does not reside in you, you are under God's wrath like Esau and Edom and are hell-bound after physical death. It's that simple.

How can you be certain that the Spirit of Christ is living inside of you?

Have you ever confessed to God that you are a sinner and incapable of saving yourself? That you believe He sent His son Jesus Christ to earth to die upon a cross, shedding his blood for your sins. That Jesus took the punishment of death you deserved. That you believe God raised Jesus from the grave after three days to prove that Jesus sacrifice was accepted. Have you asked Jesus to save you and forgive your sins? If not, stop reading and do it now.

"⁶ Esau saw that Isaac had blessed Jacob and sent him away to Padan Aram to take himself a wife from there, and that as he blessed him, he gave him a charge, saying, "You shall not take a wife from the daughters of Canaan," ⁷ and that Jacob had obeyed his father and his mother and had gone to Padan Aram. ⁸ **Also Esau saw that the daughters of Canaan did not please his father, Isaac.** ⁹ So Esau went to Ishmael and took Mahalath the daughter of Ishmael, Abraham's son, the sister of Nebajoth, to be his wife in addition to the wives he had." **Genesis 28:6-9**

Esau married descendants of Canaan, the son of Ham, the son of Noah who was cursed by God! Why were they a grief to Isaac and Rebekah? The Canaanite people were pure evil! They worshipped idols that they brought with them, were immoral, and were sexually perverted. Homosexuality ran rampant among the tribes. The people of Sodom and Gomorrah were Canaanite descendants.

Esau then attempted to correct this error by marrying one of Ishmael's daughters, but it was too late. The Lord had already closed the door of the ark. Jesus had already raptured the church pictured in the bodily rapture of Enoch.

CHAPTER 6

THE MARRIAGE FROM HELL

No, I am not speaking about yours. Remember, the Lord hates divorce. True marriage is when a man loves his wife like Christ loves the Church and gave himself for her. True marriage is when a woman has a husband like that, then she honors and respect him. Divorce will never be an option for a couple like that. Listen to the Lord of hosts.

[16] "For the LORD God of Israel says That He hates divorce, for it covers one's garment with violence," says the LORD of hosts. "Therefore, take heed to your spirit, that you do not deal treacherously." **Malachi 2:16**

The marriage from hell goes back to the "days of Noah" and what happened in those days. It was the devious plan of the devil to corrupt all flesh, thereby thwarting the plan of God to send a redeemer through the seed of the woman. The sons of God, angels, became intimate with the daughters of men, who gave birth to demonic-filled men. The NKJV of the Bible calls them giants, but the Hebrew word is Nephilim. **Gen. 6:1-13**

"[1] Now it came to pass, when men began to multiply on the face of the earth, and daughters were born to them, [2] that the sons of God saw the daughters of men, that they were beautiful; and they took wives for themselves of all whom they chose. ³ And the LORD said, "My Spirit shall not strive with man forever, for he is indeed flesh; yet his days shall be one hundred and twenty years." ⁴ There were giants on the earth in those days, and also afterward, when the sons of God came in to the daughters of men and they bore children to them. Those were the mighty men who were of old, men of renown. ⁵ Then the LORD saw that the wickedness of man was great in the earth, and that every intent of the thoughts of his heart was only evil continually. ⁶ And the LORD was sorry that He had made man on the earth, and He was grieved in His heart. ⁷ So the LORD said, "I will destroy man whom I have created from the face of the earth, both man and beast, creeping thing and birds of the air, for I am sorry that I have made them." ⁸ But Noah found grace in the eyes of the LORD. ⁹ This is the genealogy of Noah. Noah was a just man, perfect in his generations. Noah walked with God. ¹⁰ And Noah begot three sons: Shem, Ham, and Japheth. ¹¹ The earth also was corrupt before God, and the earth was filled with violence. ¹² So God looked upon the earth, and indeed it was corrupt; for all flesh had corrupted their way on the earth." **Genesis 6:1-12**

These were the demonic offspring of the angels that left their first estate and became intimate with women. They corrupted the flesh or the gene pool. Only Noah's line was not corrupted. Therefore, God said of Noah that he was perfect. Basically, his genetics were not corrupted by the Nephilim gene. Remember, God said that our bodies, the way he designed them, are the temple of the Holy Ghost. It was a body in which the Messiah would indwell. That's what the devil was attempting to stop.

These demonic offspring did horrible things.

1. They took the women hostage—this kept normal men from having children.
   a. "^{1} When human beings began to increase in number on the earth and daughters were born to them, the sons of God saw that the daughters of humans were beautiful, and they married any of them they chose. ^{3} Then the LORD said, "My Spirit will not contend with humans forever, for they are mortal; their days will be a hundred and twenty years." The Nephilim were on the earth in those days, and also afterward, when the sons of God went to the daughters of humans and had children by them. They were the heroes of old, men of renown." **Genesis 6:1-4**

   Notice that it was not until after this demonic invasion that God declared that His Spirit will not contend with humans forever. Until that time, people lived for hundreds of years, but this caused the Lord to dramatically shorten their days. Ask yourself: How did the Spirit of God contend with humans?

   It was through the preaching of Enoch and Noah. Do you know who the first prophet God called into service was?

   I'll give you a hint, it was not a Jewish prophet. It was Enoch. Jude said concerning Enoch,

   "^{14} Now Enoch, the seventh from Adam, prophesied about these men also, saying, "Behold, the Lord comes with ten thousands of His saints, ^{15} to execute judgment on all, to convict all who are ungodly among them of all their ungodly deeds which they have committed in an ungodly way, and of all the harsh things which ungodly sinners have spoken against Him." **Jude 1:14-15**

Jude made it seem as though Enoch was talking about the men of his day. Well, he was in a sense because the same evil spirits were working in both their lifetimes. Noah preached righteousness for 120 years without one convert. We preach for forty-five minutes and get upset if unbelievers do not come forward.

"⁴ For if God did not spare the angels who sinned, but cast them down to hell and delivered them into chains of darkness, to be reserved for judgment; ⁵ and did not spare the ancient world, but saved Noah, one of eight people, **a preacher of righteousness**, bringing in the flood on the world of the ungodly;" **2 Peter 2:4-5**

2. They killed, ate, and drank the blood of men—they were cannibals.

"³² And they spread among the Israelites a bad report about the land they had explored. They said, "The land we explored devours those living in it. All the people we saw there are of great size. ³³ We saw the Nephilim there (the descendants of Anak come from the Nephilim). We seemed like grasshoppers in our own eyes, and we looked the same to them." **Numbers 13:32-33**

Historians state that the Canaanite people were eaten up with venereal diseases, especially in Jericho, Sodom, Gomorrah, and the surrounding cities in the plains.

3. They committed bestiality, thereby corrupting the flesh of animals. This was to stop the sacrifices and keep man from worshipping the one true God. What the devil failed to understand was the grace of God.

   a. "[8] But Noah found favor in the eyes of the LORD. This is the account of Noah and his family. [9]Noah was a righteous man, blameless among the people of his time, and he walked faithfully with God." **Gen. 6:8-9**

The Lord only needed one man to keep his promise of a coming Messiah. God selected the animals that were not corrupted and sent them to Noah's ark.

1. The Nephilim appeared after the flood. Once again, the devil attempted to thwart God's plan by planting the Nephilim seed within the Canaanites. Notice how the devil changes his scheme as the plan of God is unfolded. After Adam fell and prior to the flood, Satan spread a wide net by attempting to pollute every creator. Once the Lord God announce His plan to use Abraham by giving him the land of the Canaanites, there was no need to pollute the entire human race or the animals. Satan focused solely on the Canaanites in hopes that when the promise came to fruition, he would be prepared to destroy the seed of the Messiah.

   God told Abraham that he was going to give him the land of the Canaanites, but it would be 400 years later because the sins of the Ammonites were not yet full.

   "[16] But in the fourth generation they shall return here, for the iniquity of the Amorites is not yet complete."
   Genesis 15:16

God would send Abraham's decedents to Egypt for 430 years, where his seed would multiply and grow into a great nation, but the devil heard this plan too.

"[12] Now when the sun was going down, a deep sleep fell upon Abram; and behold, horror and great darkness fell upon him. [13] Then He said to Abram: "Know certainly that your descendants will be strangers in a land that is not theirs, and will serve them, and they will afflict them four hundred years. [14] And also the nation whom they serve I will judge; afterward they shall come out with great possessions." **Genesis 15:12-14**

The devil focused his attention on Egypt first by enslaving God's people, then instructing Pharaoh to kill all the Hebrew male children in an attempt to kill the Messiah. Yes, the devil listens and believes the word of God though he cannot understand it because only the Holy Spirit can give understanding, and He only gives it to those who are the children of God and obey Him.

"[22] So Pharaoh commanded all his people, saying, "Every son who is born you shall cast into the river, and every daughter you shall save alive." **Exodus 1:22**

When that failed, he turned his attention to the Canaanites through the Nephilim gene to prevent the promised Messiah from being born. He would kill them through war or intermarriage, thereby polluting the genetic line. Remember, the children of Israel encounter the children of Anak, whom Joshua and Caleb expelled from the land; however, some of them managed to escape, a remnant that found a refuge in the cities of Gaza, Gath, and Ashdod.

"²² None of the Anakim were left in the land of the children of Israel; they remained only in Gaza, in Gath, and in Ashdod." **Joshua 11:22**

The Philistine giants whom David encountered were descendants of the Anakim.

"¹⁵ When the Philistines were at war again with Israel, David and his servants with him went down and fought against the Philistines; and David grew faint. ¹⁶ Then Ishbi-Benob, who was one of the sons of the giant, the weight of whose bronze spear was three hundred shekels, who was bearing a new sword, thought he could kill David. ¹⁷ But Abishai the son of Zeruiah came to his aid, and struck the Philistine and killed him. Then the men of David swore to him, saying, "You shall go out no more with us to battle, lest you quench the lamp of Israel." ¹⁸ Now it happened afterward that there was again a battle with the Philistines at Gob. Then Sibbechai the Hushathite killed Saph, who was one of the sons of the giant. ¹⁹ Again there was war at Gob with the Philistines, where Elhanan the son of Jaare-Oregim the Bethlehemite killed the brother of Goliath the Gittite, the shaft of whose spear was like a weaver's beam.²⁰ Yet again there was war at Gath, where there was a man of great stature, who had six fingers on each hand and six toes on each foot, twenty-four in number; and he also was born to the giant. ²¹ So when he defied Israel, Jonathan the son of Shimea, David's brother, killed him. ²² These four were born to the giant in Gath and fell by the hand of David and by the hand of his servants. **2 Samuel 21:15-22**

CHAPTER 7

SLEEPING WITH THE ENEMY

Remember, the Canaanites were also the people who founded Sodom and Gomorrah and all the cities within the plain that God destroyed with fire and brimstone due to their immense wickedness. Instead of remaining with the people of God to whom was promised the land of the Canaanites, Esau joined the wicked Canaanites in direct opposition to God. Esau's offspring followed in his footsteps and became even more wicked than their father.

"⁷ All your allies will force you to the border, your friends will deceive and overpower you, those who eat your bread will set a trap for you, but you will not detect it." **Obed. 1:7**

God said that Edom made a confederacy with other nations that hated Israel, in particular Babylon. Babylon was growing into a world power and had already conquered the Egyptians. They sent spies pretending to be friendly messengers to uncover ways to climb Mount Seir, where Edom resided in rock-hewn cities (see the city of Petra) and destroy the Edomite nation. The Babylonians did the same with Judah and King Hezekiah, who foolishly showed them all of Judah's treasure. The Babylonians talked the Edomites into aiding them in conquering Judah but did not realize that was part of Nebuchadnezzar's evil plan, to get the men to leave the fortified cities, kill them in route to battle, then raid the defenseless nation.

But God said to Edom concerning how He would use Babylon to destroy them, "⁸ Shall I not in that day, saith the LORD, even destroy the wise men out of Edom, and understanding out of the mount of Esau?" **Obed. 1:8**

Now, what were the hidden things of Edom to make God pronounce "⁹...and thy mighty men, O Teman, shall be dismayed, to the end that every one of the mount of Esau (Mt. Seir) shall be cut off by slaughter." **Obed. 1:9**

You may ask: Who is Teman?

Teman was a city named after Esau's grandson, son of Eliphaz.

"⁹ And this is the genealogy of Esau the father of the Edomites in Mount Seir. ¹⁰ These were the names of Esau's sons: Eliphaz the son of Adah the wife of Esau, and Reuel the son of Basemath the wife of Esau. ¹¹ And the sons of Eliphaz were Teman, Omar, Zepho, Gatam, and Kenaz." **Genesis 36:9-11**

Eliphaz and Reuel were children of Esau's Canaanite wives, the wives who grieved Isaac and Rebecca because of their idolatry and wickedness.

It begins in the next verse; "¹⁰ Because of the violence against your brother Jacob, you will be covered with shame, you will be destroyed forever." **Obed 1:10**

You may say: But wait a minute; he did not fight against the children of Israel when they came out of Egypt.

No, he did not, but God is not talking about when Israel was journeying from Egypt to the Promised Land. Beginning at verse 11, we read:

"¹¹ On the day you stood aloof while strangers carried off his (Judah) wealth and foreigners entered his gates and cast lots for Jerusalem, you were like one of them. ¹² You should not gloat over your brother in the day of his misfortune, nor rejoice over the people of Judah in the day of their destruction, nor boast so much in the day of their trouble. ¹³ You should not march through the gates of my people in the day of their disaster, nor gloat over them in their calamity in the day of their disaster, nor seize their wealth in the day of their disaster. ¹⁴ You should not wait at the crossroads to cut down their fugitives, nor hand over their survivors in the day of their trouble." **Obediah 1:11-14**

The Edomites joined with Nebuchadnezzar in invading Jerusalem. Their brutality toward the people of Jerusalem and their cruel actions in destroying the First Temple gained criticism from the prophets through the later eras. What did Edom do while their relative was being destroyed?

1. Acted like a Babylonian
2. Gloated at Judah's misfortune
3. Rejoiced over Judah's destruction
4. Boasted about their trouble because the Israelis subjugated them
5. They attacked them while they were down
6. While in the city, they mocked the people
7. They raided the city for any booty they could find

8. As the people fled the burning city, the Edomites killed them
9. Those they didn't kill they turned over to the Babylonians, who made them slaves

In **Psalm 137,** the Jews talk about how the Babylonians bashed the heads of babies against the stones.

"⁸ Daughter Babylon, doomed to destruction, happy is the one who repays you according to what you have done to us. ⁹ **Happy is the one who seizes your infants and dashes them against the rocks." Psalms 137:8-9**

CHAPTER 8

THE PURGE AND PROMISED RESTORATION

Now, the Lord warned his disciples against the Jewish religious rulers, saying, "[11] How is it you do not understand that I did not speak to you concerning bread? But to beware of the leaven of the Pharisees and Sadducees." **Matthew 16:11**

What was the leaven of the Pharisees and Sadducees? The leaven of the Pharisees was hypocrisy, while the leaven of the Sadducees was false doctrine.

For the Church, leaven was malice and wickedness. We are warned that if not contained and cut out, a little leaven will contaminate the entire body.

"[6] Your glorying is not good. Do you not know that a little leaven leavens the whole lump? [7] Therefore purge out the old leaven, that you may be a new lump, since you truly are unleavened. For indeed Christ, our Passover, was sacrificed for us. [8] Therefore let us keep the feast, not with old leaven, nor with the leaven of malice and wickedness, but with the unleavened bread of sincerity and truth." **1 Corinthians 5:6-8**

In one of the first letters written by the apostle Paul, he had to address some serious issues in the churches located in the area called Galatia (Galatians). Paul was literally shocked at how soon leaven, false doctrine, had penetrated the church. They became legalistic, wanting to mix law and grace. Since grace is elevated to a higher plain, love and grace versus forced obedience and death. Some Jews introduced leaven into the body, and it didn't take long until the entire church had believed a lie. Paul had to result to severe measures to restore them, asking, "Did you receive the Holy Spirit by grace or works?" Oh my, how we can easily be deceived if we are not filled with the word of God and lovingly obeying the gospel of grace. Listen to what Paul asked the Galatians.

"[7] You ran well. Who hindered you from obeying the truth? [8] This persuasion does not come from Him who calls you. [9] A little leaven leavens the whole lump." **Galatians 5:7-9**

Are you off course? Is there leaven in your life? If there is, and you don't repent and confess thereby having your feet washed by the Savior, the Lord of the Church, with the water of the word of God that leads to restoration. Leaven, sin, will grow and take over your life, ultimately leading to your death—physical death for a true believer.

Leaven was always a sign of spiritual or even physical (ethnic) impurity. Are you shocked by this comment? Well, then you obviously have not been reading your Bible enough, now have you.

"[15] Seven days you shall eat unleavened bread. On the first day you shall remove leaven from your houses. For whoever eats leavened bread from the first day until the seventh day, that person shall be cut off from Israel." **Exodus 12:15**

"²⁵ "You shall not offer the blood of My sacrifice with leaven, nor shall the sacrifice of the Feast of the Passover be left until morning." **Exodus 34:25**

"¹¹ 'No grain offering which you bring to the LORD shall be made with leaven, for you shall burn no leaven nor any honey in any offering to the LORD made by fire." **Leviticus 2:11**

Any of the sacrifices that represented Christ was to be offered without leaven. If it had leaven, that would mean that the offering would have fermented or seen corruption. Christ is holy, sinless, and did not see corruption. On the other hand, when the offering represented any of the people like the feast of weeks and thanksgiving offering, it was mixed with leaven because all the people were conceived in sin. The feast of weeks represented Pentecost, the birth of the church, sinners converted into saints.

"¹⁷ You shall bring from your dwellings two wave loaves of two-tenths of an ephah. They shall be of fine flour; they shall be baked with leaven. They are the firstfruits to the LORD." **Leviticus 23:17**

"⁵ Offer a sacrifice of thanksgiving with leaven, proclaim and announce the freewill offerings; For this you love, You children of Israel!" Says the Lord GOD." **Amos 4:5**

"²² You Samaritans worship what you do not know; we worship what we do know, for salvation is from the Jews. **John 4:22** You can replace Samaritans with any other ethnic group, and you will get the same response from Jesus. Don't let that concern you because Jesus also said this to those Jews, religious or not, who chose to reject Him.

"⁴⁴ You belong to your father, the devil, and you want to carry out your father's desires. He was a murderer from the beginning, not holding to the truth, for there is no truth in him. When he lies, he speaks his native language, for he is a liar and the father of lies. ⁴⁵ Yet because I tell the truth, you do not believe me! ⁴⁶ Can any of you prove me guilty of sin? If I am telling the truth, why don't you believe me? ⁴⁷ Whoever belongs to God hears what God says. The reason you do not hear is that you do not belong to God." **John 8:44-47**

"⁹ I know thy works, and tribulation, and poverty, (but thou art rich) and I know the blasphemy of them which say they are Jews, and are not, but are the synagogue of Satan." **Rev. 2:9**

"⁹ Behold, I will make them of the synagogue of Satan, which say they are Jews, and are not, but do lie; behold, I will make them to come and worship before your feet, and to know that I have loved you." **Rev.3:9**

My friend, God knows who truly believes in him and will raise them up that glorious day. Yet, he will punish all who despise and rebel against him with a great overthrow. They will be cast into the lake of fire, that burneth with fire and brimstone, into outer darkness where their worm will never die, and the fire is not quenched. There will be weeping and gnashing of teeth. **Rev. 20:15**

Obadiah now turns to the future tribulation where the culmination of punishment of Israel's sins and the judgment of the nations will run their course.

"¹⁵ The **day of the LORD** is near for all nations. As you have done, it will be done to you; your deeds will return upon your own head. ¹⁶Just as you drank on my holy hill, so all the nations will drink continually, they will drink and drink and be as if they had never been." **Obad. 1:15-16**

Along with many other nations, Edom will be completely destroyed and not enter the kingdom where Jesus will rule on the earth from Jerusalem. On that day, all Israel will be saved and restored as the kingdom priests of the Lord in the Millennium Temple. Israel will finally take possession of all the land promised to Abraham, Isaac, and Jacob.

"¹⁷ But on Mount Zion will be deliverance, it will be holy, and Jacob will possess his inheritance. ¹⁸Jacob (Judah, but they will be one nation called Israel) will be a fire and Joseph (Israel) a flame; Esau will be stubble, and they will set him on fire and destroy him. **There will be no survivors from Esau."** The LORD has spoken. ¹⁹People from the Negev (southern Israel) will occupy the mountains of Esau, and people from the foothills will possess the land of the Philistines (the Phoenicians, which is modern western Israel). They will occupy the fields of Ephraim and Samaria (northern Israel), and Benjamin (eastern Israel) will possess Gilead. ²⁰This company of Israelite exiles who are in Canaan will possess the land as far as Zarephath, the exiles from Jerusalem who are in Sepharad will possess the towns of the Negev. ²¹Deliverers will go up on Mount Zion to govern the mountains of Esau. And the kingdom (the entire earth) will be the LORD's." **Obad. 1:17-21**

Beloved, God has promised to Abraham, Isaac, and Jacob that their descendants will possess that land. When Israel is in the land and right with God, the people and the land are blessed. When Israel is removed from the land for rebelling against the Holy One of Israel, the people and the land become desolate. They need each other.

"¹ This is what Isaiah son of Amoz saw concerning Judah and Jerusalem: ² In the last days the mountain of the LORD's temple will be established as the highest of the mountains; it will be exalted above the hills, and all nations will stream to it. ³ Many peoples will come and say, "Come, let us go up to the mountain of the LORD, to the temple of the God of Jacob. He will teach us his ways, so that we may walk in his paths." The law will go out from Zion, the word of the LORD from Jerusalem. ⁴ He will judge between the nations and will settle disputes for many peoples. They will beat their swords into plowshares and their spears into pruning hooks. Nation will not take up sword against nation, nor will they train for war anymore. **Isaiah 2:1-4**

In closing, we see that God was just and righteous in stating he hated Esau. What then shall we conclude concerning the Lord's actions?

"¹³ Just as it is written: "Jacob I loved, but Esau I hated." ¹⁴ What then shall we say? Is God unjust? Not at all! ¹⁵ For he says to Moses, **"I will have mercy on whom I have mercy, and I will have compassion on whom I have compassion." ¹⁶ It does not, therefore, depend on human desire or effort, but on God's mercy.** ¹⁷ For Scripture says to Pharaoh: "I raised you up for this very purpose, that I might display my power in you and that my name might be proclaimed in all the earth." ¹⁸ Therefore God has mercy on whom he wants to have mercy, and he hardens whom he wants to harden. ¹⁹ One of you will say to me: "Then why does God still blame us? For who is able to resist his will?" ²⁰ **But who are you, a human being, to talk back to God? "Shall what is formed say to the one who formed it, 'Why did you make me like this?'"** ²¹ Does not the potter have the right to make out of the same lump of clay some pottery for special purposes and some for common use? [22] **What if God, although choosing to show his wrath and make his power known, bore with great patience the objects of his wrath,** prepared for destruction? [23] **What if he did this to make the riches of his glory known to the objects of his mercy, whom he prepared in advance for glory** [24] even us, whom he also called, not only from the Jews but also from the Gentiles?" **Romans 9:13-24**

Let us remember that the Lord alone is God who resides outside of time and space, nor is he a man who should lie. To understand the Lord's actions, we must see things from God's perspective, which is outlined for us in the Bible, the word of God. No amount of human education will help us understand this book. Only the Spirit of God can open our eyes and ears to see and hear the truth.

"[6] Seek the LORD while he may be found; call on him while he is near. [7] Let the wicked forsake their ways and the unrighteous their thoughts. Let them turn to the LORD, and he will have mercy on them, and to our God, for he will freely pardon. [8] "For my thoughts are not your thoughts, neither are your ways my ways," declares the LORD. [9] "As the heavens are higher than the earth, so are my ways higher than your ways and my thoughts than your thoughts. [10] As the rain and the snow come down from heaven, and do not return to it without watering the earth and making it bud and flourish, so that it yields seed for the sower and bread for the eater, [11] so is my word that goes out from my mouth: It will not return to me empty, but will accomplish what I desire and achieve the purpose for which I sent it." **Isaiah 55:6-11**

I plead with you, do not be like Esau and Edom. You cannot come to God your way; we are all filthy sinners who deserve judgment and are unworthy of his mercy. We have nothing God wants or needs. No amount of good works can pay our sin debts, and the penalty for that sin debt is death, **eternal death**. Since God is an eternal Spirit, God's eternal wrath will forever be upon the person who has sins, and all of us were born into sin. Therefore, all of us have sins. We deserve it, friend, but God, who is rich in mercy, full of compassion, slow to anger, and longsuffering, sent his Son, Jesus Christ, to pay our debt on the cross. This means that God treated Jesus as if he committed my sins and your sins, taking our sins from off our heads and placing them upon Jesus along with his eternal wrath. Jesus died upon the cross in our place, and God raised him from the dead to show that Jesus' sacrifice was an acceptable substitute as payment for our sins, providing us a living way into His presence. All we have to do is agree with God that we are wretched sinners and cannot save ourselves, repent, which means **being willing to turn** away from our wicked lifestyle, then believe and trust that Christ's death, burial, and resurrection satisfied God's holy and righteous judgment and wrath. If we truly believe and accept that, God has promised to allow us into his kingdom, saving us forever. Isn't that wonderful news, my friend! Will you trust in Jesus today? He would rather save you than judge you but make no mistake about it. If you choose not to trust in Jesus, God's holiness and righteousness demand payment for sin. You can either pay it yourself, which means death, and be cast into the lake of fire forever, or allow Jesus' death and burial to take your place. Jesus has promised to raise from the dead all who believe in him. The choice is yours today.

"[16] For God so loved the world that he gave his one and only Son, **that whoever believes in him shall not perish but have eternal life**. [17] For God did not send his Son into the world to condemn the world, but to save the world through him. [18] Whoever believes in him is not condemned, **but whoever does not believe stands condemned already because they have not believed in the name of God's one and only Son.** [19] This is the verdict: Light has come into the world, **but people loved darkness instead of light because their deeds were evil.** [20] Everyone who does evil hates the light, and will not come into the light for fear that their deeds will be exposed. [21] But whoever lives by the truth comes into the light, so that it may be seen plainly that what they have done has been done in the sight of God. John 3:16-21

The End

BIBLIOGRAPHY

All Scripture references are from:
New King James Version (NKJV)
Publisher: Thomas Nelson
Copyright: All rights reserved
Build date: Tuesday, March 5, 2019

New International Version (NIV)
Publisher: Biblica
Copyright: © 1973, 1978, 1984, 2011 by Biblica, Inc.
Build date: Wednesday, October 23, 2019

ABOUT THE AUTHOR

Kevin Madison is an author, husband, and father who has walked faithfully with the Lord for over 28 years. He is the son of the late Pastor Leroy Phillips and Billie Mae Phillips, who raised their 13 children to love and fear the God of salvation and King of righteousness.

Modeling his study pattern after his former pastor, Carl Brown of Baton Rouge, LA, and current favorite pastors, Dr. John Barnett and John MacArthur, Kevin has become proficient at dissecting the scriptures verse by verse. Greatly impacted by his affection and love for the late Dr. J. Vernon McGee, who always challenged his listeners to study the entire word of God, Kevin has written many topical articles and yet to be published verse by verse commentaries on the Old Testament prophets. He is the author of several books, including *Predestined to Hell?—Why would a God of Love Consign People to Hell FOREVER?*, *The Chastisement of the Lord—How the Lord responds when Christians Sin?*, and *America—the Judgment of Sodom and Gomorrah*. Several other upcoming titles are soon to be published, including the much-anticipated title, *Story of the Ages—God's Plan to Eliminate the Possibility of Sin*.

www.ingramcontent.com/pod-product-compliance
Lightning Source LLC
Chambersburg PA
CBHW020914080526
44589CB00011B/595